10 Little Rules for Understanding America

by
Danny Zimny-Schmitt

Copyright ©2025 by Danny Zimny-Schmitt
All rights reserved.

ISBN: 979-8-9988281-4-0

Little Rules Publishing

No AI Training: This publication may not be used to train generative AI models. The author retain all rights under copyright and expressly prohibits AI training without permission. Licensing for AI training and language model development is reserved by the author.

Other books in the 10 Little Rules Series

10 Little Rules for a Blissy Life
by Carol Pearson

10 Little Rules for Your Creative Soul
by Rita Long

10 Little Rules of Hank
by Wendy Price

10 Little Rules for Finding Your Truth
by Micki Beach

10 Little Rules for Mermaids
by Amy Hege Atwell

10 Little Rules for the Modern Southern Belle
by Beverly Ingle

10 Little Rules for Serving You
by Amy Hege Atwell

10 Little Rules for Sharing Your Story
by Frank Winters

10 Little Rules When Good Jobs Go Bad
by Kathleen Goggin

10 Little Rules for a Double-Butted Adventure
by Teri M Brown

**see all our titles at
www.10littlerules.com**

DEDICATION

To those who work hard every day keeping the American transportation system humming – from train and bus operators to the aircraft marshals to those staffing the rental car counter – my journey would not have been possible without you.

Danny Zimny-Schmitt

FOREWORD

I was introduced to Danny through Frank Winters, author of *10 Little Rules for Sharing Your Story*. Frank and his son Luke both know Danny well, and they told me about his fascinating travels to every county in the United States. What would make someone do that, spending all that time, energy and money on a challenge of this magnitude? As I got to know Danny better, I realized it wasn't just about ticking counties off the list to call it done. Rather, Danny's mission was driven by a true adventurer's soul, a highly curious brain always looking for the reasons behind the things he experiences, and the geographer's quest for understanding the relationship between people and they places they live. This book has made a profound impact on me, and I'm following his rules as I travel through this country and this world. I hope you find some meaning, some understanding, and some hope in these pages.

Carol Pearson
Founder & Publisher
Little Rules Publishing

Danny Zimny-Schmitt

CONTENTS

Introduction 15

Rule 1 — Take the Road Less Traveled 23

Rule 2 — Think Like a Local 35

Rule 3 — Read the Landscape 55

Rule 4 — Say Hello to Strangers 69

Rule 5 — Look Up 87

Rule 6 — Focus on Experiences 101

Rule 7 — Consider How Others Perceive You 115

Rule 8 — Challenge Your Biases 129

Rule 9 — Embrace the Messiness 143

Rule 10 — Share What You Learn 157

Conclusion 169

Danny Zimny-Schmitt

INTRODUCTION

"Why would you ever want to do that?"

This was the question posed by one of my friends when I first suggested I might make traveling to every county in the United States a life goal. I didn't have an answer then, but five years and 100,000 miles later, I finally do. I wanted to see every corner of America because I wanted to learn about the country I call home in the up close and personal way that reading books, listening to podcasts, or relying on anecdotes from others could not provide. There is something distinctive to being physically present in a place that cannot be replaced by words, stories, and Google Street View alone.

But still, why?

Since I was a child, I've viewed travel as an opportunity to see and learn about other places, rather than a source of leisure and relaxation. This often meant hogging the window seat from my younger brothers on family car trips or train rides, and pushing my parents to make our family vacations more active instead of a chance to kick back. What might I learn about the world peering out the window crossing the Appalachian Mountains for the first time, or about the differences between neighborhoods closer to home as I explored them by bike? This explorer perspective has always been in my heart; embarking on any bizarre-sounding travel goal is a point of intrigue. My mom and I are both on a quest to visit every national park, and one day I'd like to ride every mile in the Amtrak rail system.

How I landed on counties as a goal was closer to an accident. While taking a field course offered by the geography department during my senior year of college, my professor mentioned he kept track of every county he had ever been to. I found this tidbit interesting and, after the course, I printed off a blank map of all county boundaries in the US. I began coloring in those I'd already traveled to or through with an orange highlighter and kept careful track on each new trip I took. A few years later, while attending a geography conference and presenting my graduate school research, I met another county-counter (as I learned people like us were called) who also played a role in inspiring me to take on this unconventional challenge. I also learned of the Extra Miler Club (www.extramilerclub.com), an organization for everyone with a sense of wanderlust who hopes to travel to every county one day.

Beyond the wanderlust at the surface though, I was driven by a desire to better understand the country on a social/political level. I was blindsided by the first election of Donald Trump to the presidency and wanted to better understand what might have been behind such an underreported swing in political opinion. At a time when I saw most people doubling down on their previously held beliefs, joining the "Resistance" movement on the left, and closing off avenues for conversation, I was much more interested in making an effort to identify and discern the symptoms that had led a critical mass of Americans to support Trump. This came in the form of not blocking those on my social media who supported him, reading a lot of nonfiction to better understand right-of-center worldviews, and traveling across the country with the intent of learning from the places I was visiting.

The single most important book I read during this time was Jonathan Haidt's "The Righteous Mind" (Haidt, 2012), which carries the more intriguing subtitle "Why Good People are Divided by Politics and Religion." Drawing on extensive social science research, Haidt lays out how liberals and conservatives often arrive at their differing political views because of different underlying moral foundations. Using empirical data, he shows that liberals and conservatives view issues like fairness, loyalty, and liberty through very different lenses and, importantly, that neither lens is morally superior to the other. For me, the book was a great first foray into understanding why people widely respected in their own communities might have polar-opposite feelings on national politics – and how there really could be good people on both sides of our political divide. It was also a reminder that we humans tend to think in terms of stories rather than just dry facts and figures. As Joan Didion reminds us, "We tell ourselves stories in order to survive." (Didion, 1979). How had different people across the country come to tell themselves such different and incompatible stories?

Each of us (myself very much included) tell ourselves stories about our role in society, usually embellished to exaggerate our positive qualities while papering over our less flattering ones. I don't believe this is a character flaw; I think it's better interpreted as a reminder of our shared humanity, maybe even the result of our need to feel like contributing members of a social species. The flip side of the coin is the unfortunate rush to judge others who tell themselves different stories than we do, and this tendency is exacerbated when we live far away from those on whom we cast judgement. I took as inspiration a quote from Brené Brown: "People are hard to hate close up." (Brown, 2017). This idea reminded me over the course of my travels to always humanize others, even when the stories we tell ourselves are at odds.

Places are always a key ingredient in the stories we tell, since those interacting with each other on a regular basis are usually bound by a shared geography. Seeking to understand different places means sorting out how the climate, history, economics, and other factors all came together to create the place that exists today. There are myriad reasons why Vermont became Vermont and why Texas became Texas, and why they have each become so emblematic of wildly different social and political stereotypes in the popular imagination. I think it's very important to remind ourselves that everywhere is home to someone. Recognizing our shared humanity means understanding that the stories we tell ourselves have a direct relationship with place-based communities. And the fact that we each do live in a given place for a given amount of time is something that unites us all.

After considering the question of why I might want to travel to every county, the natural follow up question is how. There are 3,144 counties in the US, and the constraints of having a limited budget while working a full-time job (thankfully with some flexibility to work remotely) meant I needed a concerted strategy. I was vaguely familiar with the Traveling Salesman Problem – trying to find the most efficient way to travel to each of a defined list of points and then return home – and was surprised to find there still exists no efficient mathematical way to solve it. My main concern was not minimizing the exact number of miles traveled, but minimizing the amount I'd have to spend in pursuit of this goal. I did have a major leg up living in Denver, a city with a major airport near the middle of the country, as well as the home base of ultra low-cost carrier Frontier Airlines.

The adventure began in earnest after my 25th birthday, when I started my first job out of grad school and was finally old enough to rent a car. I'd traveled to a few hundred counties on various trips before turning 25, and these helped define some early small goals to chase. Referring back to my orange-highlighted county boundaries map, I saw that renting a car from Phoenix for a weekend would be enough for me to get to the half of counties in Arizona I hadn't yet been to and finish the state (there are only 15 counties in total). A long day trip to Rhode Island on a cheap Frontier red-eye flight would be enough to finish all five counties in that state, too. One county at a time, the map began to fill in. My love of the West, with its geographically large counties, made traveling to every county between I-25 and the Pacific Ocean one of my first intermediate goals, which I achieved just shy of my 27th birthday.

While I did travel to many counties around the West and Midwest in my own car, most were completed by flying out of Denver to a given city, renting a car and traveling to counties in the area for a few days before turning around to fly back home. When I had a free weekend coming up, I scoured Google Flights for a cheap roundtrip flight and an accompanying reasonably-priced car rental. I compared different itineraries with back-of-the-envelope calculations, then decided whether my next trip would find me bound for Baltimore, Charlotte, or Oklahoma City. The price of budget hotels and gas were also factored in, but these turned out to be a lot less variable based on timing compared to airfare and rental car costs.

My ambitious monetary goal, which I succeeded in maintaining, was to spend an average of only $10 per county visited. Some were cheaper, especially when I drove my own car from home, and some were more expensive, especially in Alaska and Hawaii – the total dollars spent ended up being in the neighborhood of $25,000 over five years. In terms of time spent, it amounted to an average of about one long weekend every month for five years plus a few full weeks visiting remote parts of the US like Alaska – along with a significant amount of planning time. Using both road atlases and Google Maps, I became adept at plotting creative routes across the country that included interesting roadside stops while maximizing the number of new counties I could check off my list.

This book is an attempt to share what I learned on my journey to almost every corner of America. There were plenty of differences, a lot of similarities, and a lot of space for nuance in between. Stereotypes proved true and were transcended; my preconceived notions were confirmed and were challenged; and I found myself coming back to the same realization over and over again as the mosaic that is America unfolded mile by mile: It's a big and complicated country out there. These are my 10 little rules for helping us all understand it a little bit better.

Danny Zimny-Schmitt

RULE 1
Take the Road Less Traveled

I am certainly not the most well-traveled American. I know many others, even those my own age, who have taken more flights, spent more time exploring beautiful places, and deeply understand places across this country that I probably never will. My goal in traveling to every county was not to break a travel record, but rather to make a conscious effort to visit places far from the tourist trail. I've been to rural North Dakota a few different times as part of this journey, but have yet to visit Disney World, and I think this has made all the difference.

One of the first things I began noticing while spending time on the road is how much tourism can affect and even change the character of a place. I love a jaw-dropping landscape, a beautiful beach, or a vibrant city as much as the next traveler but quickly came to see that places frequented by tourists are among the most difficult places to make sense of the local community dynamics. When most of the local businesses are catering to tourists and many residents are priced out of the local housing market by Airbnbs or higher rents, there may be more opportunity to recreate, but less opportunity to understand the place you're visiting.

The main tourist drag on the Hawaiian Island of Oahu is Waikiki Beach, a roughly one-mile stretch of waterfront on the east side of Honolulu. Large hotels filled with tourists from the mainland, convention halls and ballrooms crowded with conference-goers, and ABC convenience stores hawking sunscreen and souvenirs are omnipresent. Just across a small bridge spanning the Ala Wai Canal lies the rest of Honolulu, separated socially and economically from the throngs of tourists who jet there each year and stay at a large American chain hotel once they land. (I was one of them, staying at the Hyatt Regency in 2022). As my friends and I spent a few days exploring Oahu, from the North Shore to Japanese gardens to boat rides, the way we moved in and out of zones catering to tourists was striking. In a place like Hawaii, where much of the economy relies on tourism, it was easy to forget that we as visitors were in the minority; so many places were designed to cater to our desires rather than to those who call Hawaii home.

I contrasted the experience of Waikiki with a different visit I made to the state, specifically to the less visited side of the Big Island. While driving from Volcanoes National Park to Kona, a friend and I got a more authentic taste for the island off the beaten track. Late one morning, we stopped at a coffee house in the small town of Naalehu, where my friend struck up a conversation with a local ranch hand. We then stopped for lunch at Big Dogs Hot Dogs, a roadside stand where the owner grills your made-to-order hot dog in front of you, and cash is the norm. Our presence was more notable in places like these because it was more novel – few tourists from the mainland talk with a ranch hand or wander far from their resorts. We lost some of the anonymity that comes with being tourists in popular places, and this led to observations and interactions with those who knew the place like the back of their hand.

The key idea here is context – how do the places in which I present myself help me better understand or learn from those with different backgrounds than mine? Generally speaking, we tend to find ourselves in more contexts with people similar to us than different than us, whether in a socioeconomic, ideological, or religious sense. There is nothing inherently wrong with this – the observation that birds of a feather flock together goes back centuries – but it does make it harder to have genuine interactions with people less similar to ourselves. When it comes to traveling, making a conscious effort to find a few places to visit off the well-trod tourist trail will create space for the observations and interactions that open yourself to new contexts.

One American author who made a point of seeking out different contexts was John Steinbeck in his book "Travels with Charley in Search of America." (Steinbeck, 1962). After living in New York City for decades, Steinbeck realized he had lost touch with the country he had written so much about in his younger years. The chronicle of the journey captured in the book takes readers from the winding roads of rural Maine across to the West Coast, then back again across the South. Missing are mentions of tourist destinations or other big cities; traveling from New York, he spent his time interacting with various parts of rural America that were the polar opposite context to his own. Depending on where you live, seeking out different contexts to visit might look very different. Between growing up in Chicago and living in Denver as a young adult, I found myself closer to being in Steinbeck's shoes when it came to seeking out different experiences.

After three days at the Hyatt Regency in Waikiki with my friends, I had the most impactful interaction of my trip with a man I met on the city bus on my way back to the airport. He was a native of Honolulu and shared how quickly rents had been rising in recent years. Gesturing at the housing stock passing by outside the window, he explained how landlords were subdividing buildings or apartments into smaller units while still charging high rents, making homeownership that much further out of reach for most. Many of his friends had joined the growing Hawaiian diaspora in Las Vegas, the choice city for many leaving the islands. While I am cautious not to be too gullible in these situations, after my trip I saw reports in AP News about the affordability crisis in Hawaii declaring that only one in five households can afford to buy a single-family home (Terrell, 2024), and an article in the New York Times about the mushrooming number of Hawaiian expats in Las Vegas (Fawcett, 2023), where homeownership was still within reach. In retrospect, I've come to see that first trip to Hawaii as a learning experience as much as a vacation.

I finished my travels to every county in a place off the beaten track rather than a more recognizable one – along the Natchez Trace Parkway that runs from southern Mississippi to just outside Nashville, Tennessee. I invited two of my friends from my geography graduate school program to join me for this final ride, largely through the Mississippi Delta and up the Parkway. They were both Northerners; I didn't expect them to hold the state of Mississippi in very high regard. Yet after a couple days of seeing the state's lush forests, gently rolling hills, and even some rocky outcrops, one of my friends declared she never knew Mississippi could be so beautiful, and might need to plan a return trip with her husband soon. To me, this is the beauty of taking the road less traveled – it invites in our capacity for wonder, for learning, and for growth. We probably won't find ourselves inspired taking the interstate, staying at familiar chain hotels, and interacting with people most similar to those in our day-to-day lives. Out on the back roads of the Big Island or in the forests of Mississippi, you never know what you might find. Could that make all the difference?

your turn...

Take the road less traveled

When was the last time you intentionally chose to take the road less traveled, whether directly related to travel or another aspect of your life? What did you learn that you weren't expecting.

It can be hard to seek out unfamiliar contexts. How did you overcome any apprehension you might have had about the decision?

What did you learn ... about others, or about yourself?

Take a few minutes now and write down your thoughts on the following journal pages.

Danny Zimny-Schmitt

10 Little Rules for Understanding America

Danny Zimny-Schmitt

10 Little Rules for Understanding America

Danny Zimny-Schmitt

RULE 2
Think Like a Local

What does it mean to think like a local? I think a good jumping-off point is noticing how visitors to the places I've lived have interacted with that place; they sometimes spend time in the same places I would, and other times hang out primarily in the places we know as tourist spots. In Chicago, one great example of a place visited predominantly by tourists is the Sears (now Willis) Tower, which offers the highest observation deck on a skyscraper in the country. I only visited once; appropriately enough, it was when my cousins from Wisconsin were visiting the city on a family vacation. A place like Navy Pier, on the other hand, provides a good mix of visitors and locals, while most neighborhoods outside of the immediate downtown area see few tourists visiting at any given time. By thinking like a local, which includes traveling the way they do, eating the way they do, spending time in the places they do, and even listening to the same radio stations they do, we can have richer cultural experiences while we travel.

The best way to lean into this rule is to take public transportation instead of taxis or Uber whenever possible. Private rides may be convenient and save time, but they are also an excellent way to wrap yourself in a cocoon and be oblivious to your surroundings. Arranged transportation robs you of the need to pay much attention, since it's the driver's job to take you all the way to your destination, rather than requiring you to actively check bus and train schedules, notice when your stop is approaching, and navigate on foot for a few blocks. Each of these three steps puts you in the mindset of thinking like locals who take transit in their city – with a ride or two, you learn what works well and what doesn't, and can strike up conversations with people who would otherwise remain strangers on the other side of the Uber window.

In the US, public transit often gets a bad rap for being dangerous, ferrying undesirable people who you wouldn't want to rub elbows with. While I'm not here to suggest that you put yourself in uncomfortable situations when it comes to personal safety, I am absolutely suggesting that most fears around public transportation are blown far out of proportion. If you're unsure about specific neighborhoods in a city, you can absolutely find someone who will know. Think about asking the barista or waitress; they may have even taken the bus to work that morning. Avoid the hotel concierge desks; they may have a financial relationship with a ride-hailing company and play up the unreliability or safety concerns of transit unnecessarily.

Before I turned 25 and could easily rent a car, most of my travels tended to be more urban. Even though I've never lived there, Minneapolis has always been one of my favorite cities, and I am lucky enough to have an aunt who lives there. Starting in high school, I would often make my way up from Chicago to visit her, navigating on my own from the bus or train station to her house in North Minneapolis on Metro Transit. It was on some of these trips that I began to make sense of the class and racial dynamics of a city different from my own. Observing differences outside the window as the bus traveled from the skyscrapers of downtown through a tougher neighborhood to the northwest and then into the multiracial mosaic of my aunt's neighborhood provided a lesson in urban studies that I missed whenever my aunt was able to pick me up directly and drive me up I-94, bypassing the places in between.

In Minneapolis and other cities where I took public transit (Detroit, Miami, Atlanta), I would often find myself in the position of being the only white person on the bus or train. After the initial surprise factor, it became something that didn't feel as odd to me. If anything, it helped me conceptualize how someone with a different skin color might feel surrounded by those who don't look like them. There are no easy fixes to the complex racial and class politics in both rural and urban America, but working on creating more space for interactions to take place is not a bad place to start. Places like North Minneapolis are rare examples of racially integrated middle- and working-class neighborhoods, ones that we should think more about when imagining what a more diverse version of a future America might look like.

Beyond getting around a city, there are plenty of other ways to think like a local, too. Food is an obvious place to start. While travel influencers or Google may steer you toward higher priced and less authentic options, asking locals is truly the best way to find those best spots to eat. Back in Minneapolis, Al's Breakfast in Dinkytown (www.alsbreakfastmpls.com) is one such place. The narrow storefront has a single long breakfast counter; coat hangers on the wall behind the stools highlight its unpretentiousness. A great breakfast (with coffee) can be had for a little more than $10, payable in cash only. I do enjoy a fancy and overpriced brunch with mimosas as much as the next millennial, but changing it up to enjoy a meal at a place that has withstood the test of time – Al's has been serving since 1950 – grounds me in a way the hot new brunch spot advertised on my social media feed does not.

Relying on the internet for information also has its limitations, as I learned on the trip to Mississippi. On a Saturday morning in Greenwood, my friends and I were looking for a place to get breakfast downtown. Relying on Google Maps, we found two places listed as open; when we rolled up, we found a downtown devoid of pedestrians and two locked doors where Google had promised us pancakes (one had clearly not seen life as a restaurant in a while; it was harder to tell whether the other may have been a more temporary closure). So, we left downtown for the place we knew would be open; the McDonald's at the edge of town off the state highway. There, the coffee and conversation flowed freely, and we found the Saturday morning local diner vibe that wasn't available downtown.

This experience reminded me of something I had read in Kentucky Sports Radio Matt Jones' book "Mitch, Please!" (Jones, 2020). The book recounted his travels to every county in Kentucky while he pondered running for a Senate seat there in 2020. While musing about elitism and the casual ways urban folks often mischaracterize rural places, he wrote that if you don't know that it's at the town McDonald's where locals come together to talk about the issues of the day, you are definitely an elitist.

Three years later, in Greenwood, Mississippi, I saw the truth of those words come to life; most of the patrons appeared to be from the area, often multiple generations at the table. We were the exceptions to the rule, transient people grabbing a bite on our way through the area, heading someplace else. One of my best friends, hailing from the Charlotte, North Carolina area, has similarly explained to me the way Waffle House serves as a place in the South where all races and classes enjoy meals at all hours of the day.

Grocery stores are also reliable places to get a pulse on the local community. As more grocery chains offer grab-and-go options, these stores became regular pit stops for lunch when I was on the road traveling between counties. I ran into chains I wasn't familiar with that are staples in whole regions of the country, from Food Lion in North Carolina and Virginia to Win-Co Foods in the intermountain West. The ubiquity of Walmart as a source of groceries for large swaths of rural America also became apparent as I passed through large towns and small cities – a few miles away from hollowed-out downtowns there was often a Walmart with a full parking lot, buzzing with activity. Food, whether bought and then prepared at home or eaten with family and friends at a local establishment, has always brought people together and will always be a nexus point for authentic interactions.

Then, there are times when meeting locals is closer to an accident. Driving through counties in South Texas early one December, I found myself in Cuero, where a gigantic blow-up Santa was sitting in the middle of a downtown street. Curious, I parked and walked over to find a Christmas festival, complete with bouncy houses for kids, a jewelry and craft fair, and, of course, good food. The emphasis on children's activities is what I noticed most. At home in Denver, many young adults are more likely to be raising dogs than children; making sure a street festival there is dog-friendly becomes an important consideration. Passing through the western Colorado town of Gunnison en route to a hike further north, I stumbled upon another street fest emphasizing Latin American food and music, a reminder that the Colorado High Country is home to a growing number of immigrants, often operating the ski lifts and staffing the hotels tourists rely on. Street festivals like these are some of the most authentically local places I've organically found on my travels.

Even on days when I didn't linger in local spots because of the hundreds of miles I had to drive before sunset, I found another way to connect while traveling through: local radio stations. There were pop, country, classical, and talk stations in almost every corner of the country, each with their own flair and, more often than not, local news and weather updates. Talk radio in most places struck me as a poignant reminder of how more much conservative most of the country was than the places I'd called home, as local preachers shared their views on abortion, LGBT issues, and good family values. Though none of it was particularly surprising to me, it reaffirmed that America remains very much a Christian nation at its heart. Despite the often-cited statistics about declining church attendance and questions about the role of religion in public life, the "soul of America," as invoked by Joe Biden and other politicians of our time, is still an overwhelmingly Christian one and seems poised to remain so. The absence of left-of-center talk radio was something I also found curious – yes, there is almost always a local NPR station even in rural areas, but the dial is full of conservative options by comparison.

There is a specific place reliably populated with fellow travelers rather than locals to watch out for when traveling: anywhere within a half mile of an interstate exit. Filled with familiar gas stations (Shell, Exxon, BP), chain hotels (Comfort Inn, Super 8, Best Western), and restaurants (Hardee's, KFC, Burger King), these mini-cities that animate major interstate exits are transient places. While the ample number of hotel rooms available can make rates cheap to a budget traveler like me, I minimized the time I spent in these places as much as I could. Often, the short drive to the old downtown just a few miles from the exit revealed a very different place, whether a local Main Street initiative had helped the town blossom or empty storefronts highlighted the fact that the town's center of gravity completely shifted when the interstate came through. Interstate highways, with their standard signage and familiar name brands, are built for speed, funneling travelers through places they have no intention of interacting with. Relatively short detours on state or county highways reveal an America far removed from the one encountered if you never leave the interstate corridor.

Visiting new places provides an opportunity to better understand people and places we otherwise miss. Yet, when traveling, it's too easy to spend time exclusively in places that feel familiar – opting for Starbucks coffee, eating at Subway, and getting door-to-door transportation. As a guest in a different place, I find it important to choose more local experiences, both for the opportunity to learn and to show some sense of respect to those who call this place home. In plenty of places, tourists garner a bad reputation because of the lack of respect they show to locals. An antidote to this is to think like a local does; if you make an effort to imagine yourself in the shoes of those around you, respect and understanding are much more likely to naturally follow.

Danny Zimny-Schmitt

your turn...

Think like a local

Think about a time when you chose to take public transportation in an unfamiliar, city rather than a taxi or Uber. What struck you most about the experience?

Have you ever visited the same city twice, experiencing it with a local and then again on your own or with other visitors? How did the experiences compare?

Did you feel a more authentic connection to the place when accompanied by someone who knew it?

Use the space on the next few pages to jot down your thoughts.

Danny Zimny-Schmitt

10 Little Rules for Understanding America

Danny Zimny-Schmitt

10 Little Rules for Understanding America

Danny Zimny-Schmitt

RULE 3
Read the Landscape

When I was still an undergrad taking the geography field course, my professor began a lecture by recounting a story about Alexander von Humboldt, an 18th-century German naturalist and explorer. As the story went, von Humboldt, upon learning he was in the presence of a geographer, gestured to the landscape they were traveling through and instructed the geographer to "read." The concept – that human and natural history exist on the natural landscape and can be read and interpreted by us today – was a powerful one to me. I soon found myself taking it up as a personal challenge, both for the rest of the field course and in my subsequent travels across America in the years to follow.

How can we read a landscape when there are no words? The answer is vigilant observation of how landscapes change from place to place. Think about the differences between the parts of rural America immediately next to interstate highway exits compared to rural places further away. In the former, large corporate entities made significant investments that make cross country travel seamless; in the latter, there is less uniform corporate investment and more preservation of local character and unique history. Both rural and urban America are full of these local variations, and it doesn't require a geography degree to read.

Growing up in Chicago, then moving to Denver for school and work, I held the immature idea that rural America was just a giant swath of farmers and agriculture. I believed rural America was comprised solely of places in the "great in-between" I saw from the window of my Amtrak train while crossing Iowa or Nebraska on my trips back and forth. It was only when I started spending more time traveling specifically to rural counties that the diversity of the landscape became real – and more readable. I initially focused on traveling through the rural West, fascinated by the wide open spaces, vast deserts, and formidable mountain passes. Local economies depended largely on resource extraction, tourism, and occasionally agriculture wherever good soil and water were available. This almost empty landscape in parts of the West stood in stark contrast to the counties I'd eventually drive through further east in Indiana and Virginia, where rolling green hills and farmsteads, small homes and mailboxes lined most roads. This eastern rural environment, with its relatively high population density and towns every few miles, was straight up crowded compared to the rural West. Gas stations and Dollar Generals dotted the landscape; there was little need to worry whether there would be a place to gas up in the next hour, an ever-present concern in rural reaches of Idaho or New Mexico.

While the differences I've pointed out here fall under the category of human geography, there is an underlying dimension of physical geography as well. Much of the West is inhospitable to farmstead agriculture, making its settlement more dependent on government-funded water projects, mining or resource extraction, or ranching that requires far more acreage to support animal husbandry that it would further east. Historically, population densities were lower in the West because of the underlying climate and only reached higher densities around specific mine sites that offered economic opportunity, or in valleys that could support consistent agriculture following large-scale damming projects. Tourism grew, too, but again was clustered around specific sites like ski resorts, national parks, or natural hot springs, rather than being more uniformly distributed. The physical landscape thus shaped what the human landscape would later come to resemble.

The Appalachian region also faced the challenge of not being able to support the small-scale agriculture that much of the East and Midwest could, due to its poorer rocky soils; distinctly different history is still visible and readable on the landscape there today. My time spent driving on the backroads of West Virginia taught me how population patterns in the hollers tended to reflect the sites of major coal mines across its history, rather than agriculture, dispelling the false notion I had that farmers and agriculture defined rural America wherever enough rain fell. Reading about the history of West Virginia later in a book I picked up at a Charleston bookstore made me realize something else: The landscape of Appalachia had also defined the state's politics. With economic power in the state distributed amongst the relatively few hands of the mining companies rather than amongst the much larger number of farmers, West Virginia history was characterized by greater inequality and violence than neighboring Ohio or other nearby states. West Virginia was functionally an internal, extractive colony – a point that Appalachian author Barbara Kingsolver has discussed in interviews (Klein, 2023).

I began thinking about how history has ways of repeating itself as I traveled through places I'd seen written up recently by environmental publications as examples of today's extractive zones. From the Bakken Formation in North Dakota to the Permian Basin in West Texas and New Mexico, the boom in US oil production since the advent of widespread hydraulic fracturing technology ("fracking") in the early 2010s transformed geopolitics. While making the country less dependent on foreign oil, fracking has transformed the communities that find themselves on top of these oil plays. Driving through these places had me more on edge than normal, as I was sharing state and county highways with big rigs hauling equipment or other materials to well sites stretched across thousands of square miles. Towns I stopped in often had a man-camp kind of feel; because the price of labor was at a premium, people frequently moved from all over the country to take jobs in the oil patch. Room rates at basic roadside motels came at a high premium relative to places just beyond the drilling areas, so I rarely spent the night.

The question remains: Were these places better characterized as sacrifice zones or opportunity zones? In one of his State of the Union addresses, Barack Obama told the story of a man who moved west to Williston, North Dakota, to earn money to support his wife and children back in Minnesota; at the same time, left-of-center news reports tended to focus on drinking water pollution, earthquakes resulting from the extraction process, poor labor conditions, and the social tension between those who had been living in these communities for generations and the new, predominantly young male arrivals.

While I was driving through these places, one thing did become clear, particularly around the Permian and in the Eagle Ford oil play south of San Antonio: The places where all the new workers were living was completely divorced from the existing towns in the region. New modular home units sprouted up in man camps seemingly at random, set back from the highway in the middle of fields, while the small towns dotting that landscape were filled with vacant storefronts and homes that appeared to be falling into disrepair. Despite the surrounding area being flush with oil money, towns sitting on top of the oil suffered from disinvestment. The laborers in the oil patches didn't bring their families with them and raise the next generation in town; they sent their money back to where they had come from. The oil patch tended to feel more like an extractive zone than something that would help bring these parts of rural America back to life. Indeed, in a town not far from an oil play in northeast Utah, the plastic letter-board sign outside of the local bar read, "Hard times call for hard liquor."

    I did a lot of driving around the rural Midwest in the summer of 2020. My motivation was twofold. For one, I wasn't allowed anywhere near my office due to the pandemic and was going stir crazy in my small apartment; solo road trips were at least somewhat acceptable. Secondly, I adamantly wanted to correctly predict the outcome of the 2020 election, since I didn't want to wake up the morning after in a state of disbelief the way I did in 2016. I spent time plotting a multi-week route through all the corners of Michigan, Wisconsin,

Minnesota, and Iowa that I hadn't yet ticked off my list, and began tallying the number of Trump-Pence and Biden-Harris signs I saw driving through the state. There were far more Trump signs; I expected this given my rural route. I wasn't expecting where the yard signs were. As I drove along the highway paralleling the shoreline of Lake Huron (the thumb of the Michigan mitten), counting the throngs of Trump and Biden signs staring each other down across the highway, I was surprised to see the Biden signs were all on the lakefront properties while the Trump signs were all on the inland side.

I came to my initial political understanding during the Bush and Obama presidencies, and always thought it was the Republicans who owned the larger homes on the more desirable property, while the Democrats were working people with less material wealth. This drive was turning that supposition on its head – and when I finally swung over to the Lake Michigan side of the state, the story was exactly the same. Waterfront property owners were supporting Biden, and everyone inland was for Trump. As I continued my journey west toward Minnesota, the story repeated itself. While the growing divide in educational attainment between voters supporting Democrats and those supporting Republicans had been identified by 2020, the income divide was still newer and really only became incontrovertible following the more recent 2024 election. By reading the landscape of the upper Midwest, I learned this news five years early.

For all the signs that made sense, there were also plenty that left me scratching my head. In Kentucky, I saw a flag planted in someone's front yard that was half American, half Confederate, the red and white stripes on the left half fading into the angled bars on the right half. On the same trip through the Midwest where I counted political yard signs, I also spotted the stars and bars flying on private property in a number of places across the upper peninsula of Michigan. I was familiar with the line of argument that flying the Confederate flag down south amounts to "heritage not hate," yet in Michigan I saw no way around the fact that it represents hate, not heritage. Up in Sitka, Alaska, I snagged a picture of the green cross street sign where Jeff Davis Street and Lincoln Street meet. Beyond the old tensions of the Civil War, America's Christian heart also seems to be at odds with itself. So many stretches of road feel like advertising competitions between those encouraging us to turn to Jesus to avoid eternity in hell and those advertising Lion's Den or other adult stores. For good measure, the last billboard in the set reminds us the fetal heartbeat starts at five weeks.

In small and mid-sized cities, one of the most encouraging signs was to find a riverwalk or similar centralized pedestrian-friendly place that anchors the downtown. For cities that have cleaned up their riverfronts, these walkways add life to business districts in the same way Main Street initiatives can. In Sioux Falls, South Dakota, the riverwalk features footpaths around the waterfalls in the river and onward toward breweries and restaurants in the adjacent downtown area, linking the two areas together. A convention center and events space in South Bend, Indiana connects the riverwalk and downtown there. The potential for creating vibrant riverwalks is strong, as many cities grew up along rivers. Even places where the main downtown districts are not immediately on the water can take advantage of a riverwalk idea by investing in car-free pedestrian malls. Whether in car-centric Boise, Idaho or car-phobic Boulder, Colorado, these malls create a natural hub for local commerce that maximizes the ability of businesses to cluster together; since they aren't separated by large amounts of surface parking, moving between these spaces becomes easier.

Creating inviting downtown spaces is not limited to smaller cities and towns either. The third and fourth largest cities in the US (Chicago and Houston, respectively) have taken very different approaches to their downtowns, and have seen very different results. Chicago's downtown is anchored by large parks lining the lakefront and a vibrant riverwalk that stretches inland. With a blend of tourists and businesspeople, the downtown core supports local businesses throughout the day and on weekends. In Houston, the downtown area lacks a dedicated pedestrian zone and, while it is populated by businesspeople all day, it empties out weekday evenings as workers commute home. Many local businesses do not even open on weekends, since there is not enough foot traffic to support them. This is an important reminder that it's not simply the size of the city that determines what makes a vibrant downtown, but how well that space is designed to be as inviting as possible.

Beyond the examples I encountered in specific places, there were some landscape-reading universals that also became apparent as I continued to drive. Social class was always evident on the landscape. No matter how poor a county is, I would always spot a big house on top of a hill, or a sprawling McMansion with its various wings and well-kept picture windows with a new car sitting proudly in the driveway. Poverty was also evident everywhere, from poorly maintained houses and apartments to the obvious deferred maintenance in the public sphere. Showcasing material wealth seems to be something that transcends the urban-rural divide. Even in places we pass through, the ability to find an outlet to charge our phones can serve as a proxy for class. In a Greyhound station, waiting for an open outlet can be an ordeal, while in an airport lounge, there are more than enough to go around. Amtrak stations and general boarding areas at airports are usually somewhere in between.

The human desire to recreate in the places we call home was also evident everywhere. Whether it's pleasure craft bobbing at the end of docks in lakes or reservoirs, full parking lots at trailheads on state and national public lands, or state wildlife areas open to anglers and hunters, people using the land in their neck of the woods was a constant. The Christian cross was also ubiquitous, and not just at the churches that dotted the rural landscape, whether in Alabama or Vermont. I would see it at cemeteries, on billboards, and at impromptu roadside memorials for those who lost their lives on blind curves or to drunk driving. A framed quotation hanging on the wall at a coffee shop in the South even declared, "All I need today is a little bit of coffee and a whole lot of Jesus."

Reading the landscape does not require a specific skillset other than keen observation and an interest in putting pieces of the puzzle together to better understand the complex whole. Once you start reading, it will be hard to stop.

Danny Zimny-Schmitt

your turn...

Read the landscape

Was there ever a time you saw something while traveling that was initially confusing but you later came to understand? What did you learn during the process?

What do you think a visitor to your hometown would read on the landscape? Do you think their observations would be accurate?

How will you look at your next travel destination in an attempt to read the landscape?

Use the journaling space on the following pages to write your thoughts.

10 Little Rules for Understanding America

10 Little Rules for Understanding America

Danny Zimny-Schmitt

10 Little Rules for Understanding America

RULE 4
Say Hello to Strangers

When I was growing up, my grandma would always warn me about "stranger danger," and I took her words seriously. By the time I made it to middle school, I began to embrace my introverted side more fully and found little reason to talk to friends, let alone strangers. It still feels a bit out of character for me now to advocate for something relatively new to me. Sometimes the best place to say hello was commiserating over a shared travel delay (late train, cancelled flight); other times it was at the local bar or coffee shop. Over time, I found myself more willing to be the one to initially break the ice, find a point of common ground, and have a meaningful conversation.

One of my favorite places to say hello is the sightseer lounge car on long distance Amtrak trains. Open to First

Class and Coach passengers alike, lounge cars reflect a cross-section of America, with both people who live in the immediate area and might be taking the train just a hundred miles and people passing through the state on their way to somewhere else. When I had just started college and was equally excited and unsure about what the future might hold, I struck up a conversation with an older man on a train across West Texas. After the default questions that often kick off a conversation in the lounge car (where are you from, where are you going, how's the train ride been), he asked me about the book I'd been reading. I shared that I really enjoyed reading and writing in my free time but was hesitant to pursue a real career in writing or journalism because of concerns about being able to find a decent paying job in the field. He then started telling me about his work in the oil refineries outside of Beaumont, Texas. While he hadn't found the jobs he'd worked on personally fulfilling, he felt that his work had at least offered enough stability to raise a family. As I launched into another round of concerns about jobs, his advice to me was simple: "Become a writer, dude."

Buses, whether intercity or local, were another place I was easily able to connect. Beyond shared musings about delays, conversations I had on buses were pointed reminders of the privileges I enjoyed and tend to be oblivious to in my day-to-day life. A young man – my seat mate on a Greyhound ride from Amarillo, Texas, to Tulsa, Oklahoma, on his way to see his grandma in

Joplin, Oklahoma – explained to me how he saved money on food while traveling: He would buy two orders of fries rather than fries and a burger because he could fill up just on fries and save a few dollars. Folks in the process of moving their lives across the country, their possessions in the backpacks and overstuffed duffels spilling into the seat next to them, might be moving out to try to make it on their own, or moving back after their dreams in California didn't come to pass. Unlike Amtrak passengers, most of whom mentioned cars back home, it was my impression that many bus riders have no access to a car. This pushed me to ponder the severe mobility limitations of Americans who don't drive, and how much slower and more difficult travel can be for them.

In Rhode Island, a statewide public bus system called RIPTA connects the urban and rural parts of the smallest state in the country. Riders on these buses included those who lived too far to walk to the closest stores and were hauling their groceries home as well as students without cars traveling to their college campus. Amongst the drivers and some of the regular passengers, I heard an unmistakable twangy accent (my friend from the state simply calls it the Rhode Island accent) that has long disappeared from the places where tourists are likely to find themselves yet persists in places where locals still dominate. In other states, I also found myself riding various shuttles that might connect stores like Big Lots and Kroger at the edge of town to the higher density residential areas as I tried to navigate non-urban America without a car.

In Michigan, I called the Blue Water Transit agency help center while struggling to find the bus stop for a shuttle from the northern Detroit suburbs to Port Huron. In a thick Upper Midwestern accent, they told me the stop was located just outside of Bagger Joe's (BAY-ger Joe's), a restaurant that was now permanently closed but evidently still a local landmark. On other local shuttles run by towns or small city transit agencies, I listened as passengers casually chatted with the driver they clearly knew well from repeated rides. Town gossip was exchanged; which of their mutual friends had been taken to jail last and who had recently broken up or got together were among the topics discussed. Talking with strangers also served as a reminder that I could very much feel like an outsider in my own country when I veered off the more well-trod track.

On the rare occasions I took a cab, I found them to be places where I could have very candid conversations with the driver who usually had an uncanny knack for understanding the places where they drove for a living. In many ways, taxis provide a unique low-stakes environment for an honest conversation or sharing a hot take. Since the relationship is inherently transactional and won't last more than a few minutes, there is less pressure to say something that the other person wants to hear than there is in a community context. While traveling in Miami during Trump's first term, I had an Uber driver who was a recent immigrant from Argentina. I was with my dad on that trip, and he asked the driver what he thought about Trump's politics. To our shock, he explained he didn't see anything wrong with Trump, that he was simply a man who loved his country and was doing the best he could by it. I read this as an early indicator of Trump's growing support from communities where you wouldn't expect it. Seeing how the profile of Uber drivers has changed from its early days to the present has been telling as well. Back in 2015, I recall many conversations with drivers who explained they were driving on the side to earn a little extra money to spoil their grandkids. On more recent trips, I've had many conversations with drivers, often recent immigrants themselves, who work full time or more, sometimes in vehicles leased to them by the company.

Of course, interactions with strangers were not uniformly positive. Sometimes, those who come up to you on the street or at a terminal put on false pretenses or friendliness in a disguised attempt to ask for money. These situations can get uncomfortable, as our human brains try to rapidly assess questions rooted somewhere deep in social psychology: What do I owe my fellow humans who are in a tougher place in life than I am? Sometimes I gave them something, other times I pretended to be carrying no cash. I walked into one particularly elaborate attempt on Woodward Avenue in Detroit with a young man trying to raise money to send himself to Howard University in the fall – complete with an official-looking clipboard and school acceptance letter. Taken by the elaborate work involved, I gave him the same $10 others who'd signed his paper also pledged, hoping that I was paying it forward and not being played. Just as often as being asked for money, I was asked the mundane request for a cigarette, or a light for one they already had. Never a smoker myself, these requests always got the same answer from me.

On at least one specific occasion while I was county-counting, talking with strangers helped me get out of a tough situation. My flight from Dallas to Lubbock, Texas had been delayed due to thunderstorms, and wasn't arriving until after midnight. I'd planned to take an Uber to my hotel closer to downtown, but the app told me no drivers were available, even as I refreshed it time and again. Out on the curbside, no taxis were lined up either; my fellow passengers all began climbing into the vehicles of waiting friends and family. I made small talk with an older woman also standing on the curb with her suitcase waiting for her own ride, and shared my plight. When her husband pulled up, she told him that they'd be stopping to drop me off at the Microtel on their way home. Driving across the cool Texas night on I-27 in the wee hours, I thanked them profusely – and they refused to take any money for saving me from a lonely night in the Lubbock airport.

Alaska was perhaps the state where I talked with the most strangers simply because of how long it takes to get to all 30 boroughs (Alaska's equivalent of counties), most of which are not accessible by road. Even after a cruise on the Inside Passage with my grandma back in high school and during trips to far-flung national park sites with my mom after college, I was still missing so many. To avoid breaking the bank, I got a weekly rate at a hostel in Anchorage, taking the city bus to the airport each morning for day trips to Bethel, Nome, Kodiak Island, and the Aleutian Islands. Leveraging credit card signup bonuses and redemptions through Alaska Airlines' Mileage Plan program, I kept the out-of-pocket costs in the very low thousands. While my travels in most other states relied on rental cars and to a lesser extent trains and buses, I saw Alaska by ship and air, marveling at the fjords of the Southeast, the barren tundra north of the Brooks Range, and the Aleutians chain of volcanic islands outside the airplane window flying all the way to tiny Adak (which is closer to Tokyo than it is to Seattle, Washington).

While taking a Ravn Alaska flight on a prop plane to a far-away borough, I was seated next to a gentleman who worked for the Federal Aviation Administration (FAA). What was someone from the lower 48 doing so far from home in St. Mary's, Alaska? I must be visiting someone I knew who was from there. No, I explained I was trying to go to every county in the US, and this was about the only commercial flight from Anchorage to the Kusilvak borough. After I shared a primer on why I was trying to accomplish such a feat, he shared his own story. He was a specialist in airport runway lighting, so was called on by rural airports across the state when an issue arose. While he flew commercial whenever possible to save taxpayer money, some emergencies necessitated his taking charter planes on short notice. Curious, I asked how much these charters usually cost (thousands of dollars) and began to understand why a more forbidding place like Alaska might require much larger subsidies from the federal government just to (literally) keep the lights on.

In Nome, another town in the outer reaches of Alaska, famous for being the finish line of the annual Iditarod dog sled race, I spent an hour in the local visitors' center talking with the national park service staffer and a local guy who had stopped by on his lunch break. We talked about the still small but recovering number of visitors because of the pandemic (this was the summer of 2021), and I asked about a sign I'd seen at the airport noting that the short flights across the Bering Sea to Russia catering to tourists had been cancelled. He mentioned that these had been popular with tourists (Kamchatka was a lot closer to where I stood than the Anchorage hostel room where I'd woken up that morning) and was optimistic they'd be back the next summer – this never happened because of the war in Ukraine that would be raging by then. He then shared a story about a crooked local cop who had recently stopped a local young woman for dubious reasons, as rumors swirled about whether he'd demanded sexual favors in exchange for letting her go. Reports of rumors, misbehaviors, and salacious stories were universal wherever I talked with strangers.

Back in downtown Anchorage between trips, I checked out a local bar with a name that intrigued me: Darwin's Theory. Not quite a dive bar, but not quite a classy hangout either, they served free popcorn with your beer or liquor of choice. I found myself there mid-morning on a weekday before an afternoon flight talking with someone who prided himself on having been to Burning Man every year for a decade straight. He explained the whole festival was based on the barter system, and the only thing you could buy from the festival organizers was coffee. Having the right drugs (he claimed molly was especially useful) to barter was a key to having a great time. As someone whose live music experience hasn't gone much beyond the occasional show at Red Rocks, hearing the skinny about a festival more than a 50-hour drive away in the high desert of Nevada from an old pro made the massive country feel small. I closed down a bar in Sitka later that week, talking to the bartender until 2 am about how the town had completely changed over the past decade since it was discovered as a prime fishing destination by the wealthy from the lower 48. Locals were either stuck in houses that had appreciated so much in value they knew if they sold they'd never be able to afford to move back again, or they'd grown up there but had been forced to move away because they couldn't afford the rents. Some places in Alaska had been "discovered" by tourists, with many consequences for Alaskans caught in the lurch.

Coffee shops were another space I found it easy to meet strangers – and as more of a nerd than a drinker, I tended to feel more at home in them, surrounded by people with their noses in books or on laptops, than I did in bars. I made many stops in small town coffee shops to take meetings while I was working on the road, and I noticed the panoply of relatives catching up together, students at local colleges getting work done, and book clubs discussing their latest read. It was also hard not to notice how coffee shops in rural places seemed to attract a cross section of the population that isn't always representative of the local area. From my outsider perspective, coffee shops were often the liberal bastions in otherwise conservative places, with pride flags flying in their windows and a more intellectual bent to their customers. I began to recognize that spending $4 on a drip coffee or $6 on a latte can be a lot to folks trying to make ends meet, and while I found coffee shops to be the most affordable space to check out the local vibe – relative to the cost of a full sit-down restaurant meal – it's still a service at a premium compared to the coffee that might be had for just a dollar at the gas station or McDonald's. Finding myself in need of caffeine in the middle of a long drive off the tourist trail in far western Colorado, one small town had no coffee shop, but a self-serve machine advertised a large coffee for $1.49. The cappuccino machine next to it was out of order – perhaps it was a fancy feature for visitors and not locals.

At other times, I walked into situations where I found myself talking with strangers accidentally. On yet another road trip through Texas (with 254 counties, it has the most of any state), I stopped in the town of Breckenridge to check out their downtown. I wandered into the Fine Arts Center (www.breckenridgefineart.org), thinking I might find a restroom, and instead found myself led on a half-hour tour of the place by the woman staffing the front desk. Hearing I'd traveled all the way from Colorado to her town off the map, she took me through their prime exhibit on the festival dresses of Texas – a beautiful collection of dozens of intricately sewn dresses that had been designed for various festivals across the state. No expert in dressmaking myself, I let her Southern hospitality take over and inspire me to learn. I came to see this experience as representative of the journey more broadly: Sometimes you need to be willing to take a short detour from the best-laid plans, lean into the spontaneity of the moment, and say hello to a kind stranger out on the road.

Danny Zimny-Schmitt

your turn...

Say hello to strangers

It can be tough to say hello to strangers – is there a way you like to break the ice?

What is your favorite place to meet strangers? Is it an environment you're already comfortable in, or one that's new to you and you're looking to strangers to better fit in?

Has talking to strangers ever helped you out of a tough situation on the road, like what happened to me in Lubbock? Did it serve to remind you to have faith in our fellow human beings?

Use the journaling space on the following pages to write your thoughts.

Danny Zimny-Schmitt

10 Little Rules for Understanding America

Danny Zimny-Schmitt

10 Little Rules for Understanding America

Danny Zimny-Schmitt

RULE 5
Look Up

I completed the vast majority of my travels to every county between the years of 2019 and 2023, deep in the age of the smartphone. My friends and parents might tell you that I'm addicted to my phone (once when I was home for Christmas break, my mom said she didn't think I could survive 24 hours without my phone – we made a bet and I barely won), but while traveling the country I made a conscious effort to distance myself from my phone as much as I could. I generally navigated using old-fashioned paper state highway maps rather than having Google Maps tell me where to turn. By doing this, I found myself paying closer attention to the road signs and my surroundings than when I outsourced that responsibility to an automated voice. Looking up – from our phones or whatever else is distracting us – and taking care to notice and be present in the world around me was perhaps the most unexpected but important lesson learned on the road.

Except for those counties close enough to Denver to visit in my own car, most of my trips started on the train to Denver International Airport. I immediately noticed a large proportion of passengers on the train were not on the way to catch a flight but rather airport employees on their way to work. People of all races and backgrounds, speaking familiar and unfamiliar languages, crowded the train station platform at the 40th and Airport stop where I often left my car. In the predominantly white metro area that is Denver, it was an important reminder of who is doing most of the work to keep the transportation nerve center that is Denver International Airport up and running every day. It can be easy to overlook that fact if you're zipping to the airport in a private car and oblivious to your surroundings because your smartphone is zapping you with distractions.

Looking up helps you recognize more than just the people around you. With the aid of road atlases and quirky roadside guides, I began paying attention to and even detouring to cute-but-obscure markers of Americana that are the pride of towns all over what some refer to as "flyover country." Have you heard of Carhenge, the replica of Stonehenge in Alliance, Nebraska, made up of old cars? What about the statue of the world's largest turtle riding a snowmobile in Bottineau, North Dakota? Did you know that Cawker City, Kansas and Darwin, Minnesota compete for the title of having the world's largest ball of twine? (I only saw the Cawker City one, so no official verdict from me on whose is bigger). When I stopped at the Nebraska National Forest one day for a picnic lunch and a climb up its observation tower, I was left scratching my head after learning the forest had been planted *by hand* by a team from the University of Nebraska as an experiment on the feasibility of growing trees in an otherwise treeless part of the state.

Time on the road made it hard not to see the intricate web that is the American transportation and logistics system. Sharing the road with long-haul truckers, seeing the intermodal containers rolling by on trains multiple miles long, and noticing the massive Amazon distribution centers often positioned just outside major metro areas were all testaments to the miracle that delivers the goods we order to us with speed, efficiency and low costs. As an urban resident, I find it all too easy to forget just how many steps are involved in the process of fulfilling my Amazon purchase after I click "Place Order." Seeing the massive scale of the transportation and warehousing infrastructure up close – whether from the window of a train passing through a busy yard or the magnitude of truck traffic on roads anywhere near a large distribution center – were hints at the vast apparatus that makes all of it possible.

Beyond consumer goods delivered to our doorstep, there is the similarly invisible process of food making it from rural areas to our grocery shelves. After getting over my preconceived notion that rural America was just farmers wherever there was enough water to raise crops, I began to pay more attention to the nuances between different parts of our agricultural system. There were the intensely cultivated fields of Iowa run by large agribusinesses, stifling in their uniformity and perfectly straight rows of crops. There were the confined animal feeding operations (CAFOs) in the eastern Carolinas, with a smell so rancid I couldn't roll up the windows of my rental car fast enough. The wide-open rangelands of the intermountain West looked empty at first, and I needed to remind myself to be on the lookout for grazing animals that might be wandering across the roads. I saw the towns across the Great Plains anchored economically by local slaughterhouses. It's too easy to forget all of the logistical steps involved in the process of getting our dinner to our plates each night, from the vegetables grown in California's Central Valley to the grains from downstate Illinois to the beef processed by immigrants in the Oklahoma panhandle.

Much like noticing markers of class on the landscape, looking up also makes it impossible to ignore seeing class distinctions while navigating between places without a car. From Portland, Maine, to Portland, Oregon, I consistently noticed folks who were down on their luck gathered together in the same places. These places included areas surrounding major transit centers downtown, parks and green spaces adjoining these hubs, on corners with check-cashing businesses and, increasingly, outside of 7-Eleven convenience stores. As we push people living at the margins of society out of public spaces, they will go on living in whichever de facto places they are permitted to – which interestingly enough tend to be the same types of places across the whole country.

Political ideology also made appearances in unexpected places. Even when it wasn't election season, sometimes the gift shop or spirited souvenir store in tourist towns gave away the political leanings of its owners and/or the tourists who frequented the area. I spotted pot shots at Trump and jabs at anti-intellectualism on the main drags in coastal Oregon and in big cities from Seattle to New York. But Key West, Florida, during my visit in 2022 presented more of an enigma. T-shirts adorned with Trump's face read "Miss Me Yet?" reminiscent of the ones of Obama I'd seen four years earlier in Denver. "Let's Go Brandon" merchandise abounded, as well as Ron DeSantis 2024 "Make America Florida" shirts. But the words weren't uniformly conservative: Pro-gay slogans and libertarian ethos adorned the shirts, too. I overheard the Cuban owner of one of the shops discussing socialism with a like-minded customer checking out. "Every time they try socialism again, they make excuses for why it didn't work last time and promise this time they'll do it right, that it will be different this time," he sighed, shaking his head. "But every time it's the same, it just doesn't work," he continued on as the customer nodded her head in ardent agreement.

The seeming inconsistency of political opinion expressed in Key West and in other places (for example, in Central Wisconsin a Trump sign shared a farm field with a sign declaring opposition to a proposed CAFO in the area) provided concrete examples of something I'd read in books: Many Americans' political opinions don't line up neatly with the options provided by the two major political parties. In Key West, that seemed to mean pro-gay and anti-socialism. In other places, it might be pro Medicare-for-All but anti-immigration. Or American First but anti-big business. So many Americans, ideologically torn between the dominant political parties, often are the swing voters who ultimately play kingmaker in most election cycles. They are scorned by the Democratic and Republican establishments alike when they don't break their way. I think the better solution is to put in the effort to learn from them and understand why they hold the seemingly opposing views they do.

Signs of fervently holding what seem like contradictory views were evident across the old Confederacy, even a century and half after the Civil War. While official national battlefield sites from Shiloh, Tennessee to Appomattox Courthouse, Virginia tell the story written by the winners, other monuments have been built by organizations like Daughters of the Confederacy to commemorate the history of the war from another perspective. Right outside the county courthouse in Oxford, Mississippi, I spotted one of these sites. It read, "In memory of the patriotism of the Confederate soldiers of Lafayette County, Mississippi. They gave their lives in a just and holy cause." My inner Yankee, screaming in disbelief, wondered whether I could report this to the appropriate authorities for removal from the public sphere.

The rural South was probably where I had the most to learn, even if looking up sometimes made me uncomfortable. There was something haunting about seeing the cotton growing in central Georgia or the Arkansas Delta right next to the highway that carried me quietly on by. Stopping at a visitors' center in Biloxi, Mississippi, I saw a flyer for the nearby Jefferson Davis Presidential Library. While the National Voting Rights Museum in Selma, Alabama is very well done, the history it recounts is disturbing, as it reminds us that for almost two centuries of its existence, the US was not a true democracy. There was one other peculiar thing I noticed about the South: Across the region, bridges always seemed to be named after someone. I still can't make sense of why the bridges in Louisiana all need to be named after a dead politician or highway engineer, when those in Connecticut or Montana get along fine without names.

It's not my goal to demonize the South, yet I would be remiss if I didn't mention some of the other differences I encountered there. To borrow from one of its favorite sons, William Faulkner famously declared, "The past is never dead. It's not even past." (Faulkner, 1950). While there is much to be said about the universal truth expressed in his quote, it does feel somehow more applicable to the South than the rest of the country. Speaking in broad terms, other regions have seen more dramatic social and economic changes over the last century than the South has. For one, immigration to other regions has tended to be higher. Secondly, larger cities in the East and North saw massive changes from large-scale industrialization – and often, later de-industrialization – and the West was still being settled. Boston is an example of a place that has thoroughly reimagined itself from its puritanical religious beginnings to the diverse and intellectual hub it is today. Reinventions come with new architecture, economies, and attitudes. With some notable exceptions in the urban South, the region hasn't changed as quickly, making the past often feel larger on the landscape than in many other places across the country.

your turn...

Look up

Think about a time when your phone died while you were away from home. Did you find yourself paying closer attention to the people or places around you? What did you notice that you usually overlooked?

When you travel and see new things, what usually stands out to you the most?

What have you seen recently that surprised you?

Take some time to write your thoughts on the next few pages.

Danny Zimny-Schmitt

10 Little Rules for Understanding America

Danny Zimny-Schmitt

10 Little Rules for Understanding America

Danny Zimny-Schmitt

RULE 6
Stop Counting Places & Focus on Experiences

At first glance, this rule might sound a bit antithetical to the journey I took, driven by my goal of checking every single county off a list of thousands. So, this is the cheat rule in the book: If you master this one, you can maximize how much you learn from traveling even if you don't have the time or resources to crisscross the whole country. The key is to focus on having as many unique experiences as possible, irrespective of the number of states, counties, or cities you are checking off a bucket list.

In Rule 1, I used the word *context* to get at the essence of this idea. Think of context like the setting in a novel; it encompasses the place, the people, and the sounds, sights, and smells of the environment in which the novel is set. When it comes to traveling, you'll learn more staying at locally owned motels in different corners of your own state across 20 nights than you probably will spending one night in each state at a Marriott in the largest city. The same idea can be applied to taking transit through the city or suburbs that you usually only see from behind your windshield. Additionally, consider the places where you feel more at home or more like a foreigner. If you've always lived in cities, you probably have a lot more to learn from spending time in rural environments and small-town America. If you've usually lived in smaller towns, you may have a lot more to discover from exploring bigger cities.

I started learning this lesson of context by accident before I set out in earnest on my county-counting adventure. When I was still in high school, I ran a few triathlons around Chicago and southern Wisconsin. After being too distracted with my studies, internships, and jobs during college and grad school, I returned to my old hobby in the summer of 2018. Put off by the $100-$200 registration costs of triathlons along the Front Range of Colorado, I started to look for races farther away, where I could race for closer to $35. Over that summer, I traveled to Nebraska for triathlons in McCook and Sidney, and to Kansas for triathlons in Hays and Garden City.

What started as a chance to save a bit of money and drag one of my friends with me to a place neither of us had been before turned into a crash course in understanding how small towns were distinct from the cities where I'd spent my life. The first race, in McCook, was named Michelle's Triathlon (www.visitmccook.com/events/michelles-memorial-triathlon) in honor of a local woman who passed before her time but encouraged everyone to pursue their fitness goals rather than put them off. An inspirational quote from Michelle – "If not now, when?" – was included in the race materials. The swim was held in the outdoor lap pool at the local recreation center; the bike portion directed racers onto roads cutting into the wide-open plains beyond the edge of town; and the race ended with the run along a creekside trail. In this small race, there were fewer than 100 finishers, and a casual awards ceremony with lunch followed.

In Garden City a few weeks later, I ran a similar course that began and ended at the local recreation center. One of the race organizers approached me afterwards to encourage me to come back for one of the other triathlons in the southwest Kansas six-city triathlon series, which were all listed on his paper handout. Somehow, only the Garden City one had made it online where I'd found it on a national race finder website (www.runningintheusa.com). A couple of years later, I did make it back to run the race in Liberal, Kansas (making the obligatory stop at Dorothy's House and the Land of Oz). With a fast run at the end, I narrowly edged out the hometown swimming hero and was suddenly worried that I might be seen as the big city enemy who played spoiler in this local race. Instead, they were impressed I'd made the trip all the way out from Colorado to see Liberal. At a time when rural places were pilloried for being bastions of racism, misogyny, and homophobia on account of their support for Trump, my own experiences stood at odds with the media narrative.

In Rule 3, I described how riverwalks and pedestrian malls often served as focal points for commerce in small and mid-sized cities. In small and mid-sized towns, the equivalent was a strong Main Street, often the result of hard work by local boosters and successful applications for outside dollars to fund downtown improvements that in turn make them more attractive places for entrepreneurs to build businesses. There were many markers on a Main Street that I found to serve as rough proxy indicators for the economic health of the community. The base level was a restaurant and a bar or two. A local coffee shop was a level up from there, a local bakery was another. By the time you got to a bookstore or a craft brewery, the Main Street was definitely thriving, offering a host of places to eat and drink. The highest rung on the ladder was being able to support a hotel downtown.

Decorah, Iowa was one of the best downtowns I found on my travels that didn't have the advantages of being in a tourist area the way many great Main Streets out west do. I enjoyed a cup at Impact Coffee (www.impactcoffee.com), shopped at Dragonfly Books (www.dragonflybooks.com), and was sad I didn't have time to spend the night at Hotel Winneshiek (www.hotelwinn.com) — but I did add it to my bucket list for a future trip. Decorah does have two important advantages that have been found to buoy many rural places from decline, colloquially referred to as meds and eds. The local medical clinic, WinnMed, anchors the east side of town and serves the local region, while a small liberal arts college lies just across the bridge over the Iowa River on the northwest end of town.

As a budget conscious traveler, I began noticing another context – how much more expensive it was to stay overnight in walkable or downtown areas compared to motels out by the interstate. I consistently found hotel prices to be well over $100 a night in most downtowns, while being under $100 or at least close to it on frontage roads only accessible by car. Even in Decorah, a night at the hotel downtown goes for roughly double what the cheapest options along the state highway at the edge of town cost. When I was renting a car, this wasn't a major issue; I'd simply check out the downtown area and grab a bite to eat before retreating to the budget motel out by the highway. When I was traveling by bus or train, there was no way to access these hotels without walking along highways with no sidewalks (and many small towns are not reliably served by Uber). Understanding what options I had access to and their relative costs, based on my means of transportation, became an unexpected lesson along the way. In some instances, the cost of a daily rental car plus a cheaper hotel night still cost less than the hotel night alone in the walkable downtown area.

Trains and buses were the most important ways I found to access additional contexts, but for different reasons. On Amtrak, it was the opportunity to see places that couldn't be seen as easily from roads. My dad sometimes joked that riding trains provides an "armpit view of America" because of the proximity of many rail lines to old industrial areas, especially near major cities. This was true enough in many places. One place that surprised me most was the stretch along Amtrak's premier Northeast Corridor running south from Philadelphia into Delaware, where industrial decay and rundown neighborhoods stand in sharp contrast to the sophisticated, urban downtowns those high-speed trains are whisking us between. It's important to remind ourselves that these places do exist even when it's easy to ignore them as places we don't see outside our train or airplane window. They are still home to our fellow citizens.

The context differences were more class-based when it came to bus travel. Whether intercity carriers like Greyhound or local transit authorities, buses often have a negative reputation because it's often how the most disadvantaged among us get around with some degree of accuracy. There is probably no faster way to jump out of your normal context and rush into a new one than planning a trip of a few hundred miles or more taking only buses. While trains speed us through places we don't care to visit and planes fly us over them, buses are vivid reminders of the Americans who live in those places in between as they make their journeys with stops frequent enough to be accessible to everyone.

Making a list of places and checking them all off a list is straightforward. But what qualifies as a new context? Can it be quantified into a list, too? I think the short answer is no, but that doesn't mean it's not very real. When considering a given context, you might ask yourself how many people like you – whether that means educational or racial background, socioeconomic status, or political beliefs – are in a given environment in which you find yourself. The more people who differ from you, the more opportunities you will likely have to learn and avoid the group-think of homogenous settings. Context-hopping is uncomfortable, but it absolutely lies at the heart of personally and collectively coming to a better understanding of ourselves and others.

Danny Zimny-Schmitt

your turn...

Focus on experiences

Have you ever suddenly found yourself in a different context, either planned or unplanned?

How did you feel throughout the experience?

Is there a context you feel you don't know well but are interested in learning more about? How might you go about learning?

Write down your thoughts on the next few pages.

Danny Zimny-Schmitt

10 Little Rules for Understanding America

Danny Zimny-Schmitt

10 Little Rules for Understanding America

Danny Zimny-Schmitt

RULE 7
Consider How Others Perceive You

Up to this point, I've focused this book almost exclusively on sharing my first-person account of my travels, hopefully providing some encouragement to you to go out and better understand the country. However, we are not visitors to a zoo, map in hand moving from exhibit to exhibit studying the country like a biologist might study animals. We are visitors to other places that are home to Americans – people who will also observe, assess, and make judgments about us in the same way we do with them. Whether we are observing or being observed, there will always be imperfect judgments and misunderstandings – we are only human. By reminding ourselves of this, we might be more willing to offer ourselves and others some grace when our snap judgments are found to be wrong.

My focus on places so far means that I really haven't told you very much about myself, either. I have a background in environmental science and geography, a job that paid me enough to afford $500 a month on this pursuit across multiple years, and an interest in understanding America both theoretically and at the ground level. My motivation also comes from the economic and cultural whiplash I felt trying to reconcile the first 18 years of my life with the subsequent dozen. I grew up in a diverse neighborhood in Chicago, attending Chicago Public Schools for 14 years, from pre-k through high school. This environment provided the opportunity to learn about racial and socioeconomic diversity firsthand from a young age as I befriended classmates whose families had roots all across the world, from Palestine to the Philippines. My love for biking encouraged me to experience the neighborhoods I could reach in less than an hour on two wheels, whether they were places where most storefronts signs were in Spanish or ritzy suburbs with large homes that us city kids loved to write off as snobbish, home to aloof types who had no claim on the "real" Chicago. I made it my personal quest to explore as many places as I could, even carefully timing bike rides with high school friends through tough neighborhoods in the early morning hours when they felt safer.

10 Little Rules for Understanding America

When I began college at the University of Denver (a private institution), overnight I found myself exposed to much less diversity, with most of my new classmates and friends coming from a narrow socioeconomic band that I had never known. If I'd felt like one of the better off kids in my high school class, I now felt like one of the poorer people in my college class. I sought to understand where they were coming from, even if they mostly hailed from the exact type of suburbs my high school teammates and I had loved to judge. The anthem of my cognitive dissonance at the time was Eminem's *8 Mile Road*, a rap of his inner conflict being torn between different worlds, albeit in a more literal and existential way than my own dissonance. I spent a lot of time trying to find my voice and my footing as a white male from Chicago, which at DU was accompanied by certain stereotypes that I felt were antithetical to how I lived my life. It's not fun to be put into a box and judged quickly, no matter which box you're being put into. When you're on the road, it's helpful to be cognizant of how we are being seen by those around us – and how that may be affecting how we're being treated and the experiences we are having.

Traveling to remote national parks in Alaska was a sharp reminder of the privilege I enjoyed and may have been taking for granted, which manifested itself in the simple fact of my age. My quest to get to Katmai National Park required a commercial flight to King Salmon, a shuttle ride over bumpy roads to a water taxi, and then an hour on the water taxi itself out to the park's visitors center at Brooks Camp, far away from the nearest road. The operators of the shuttle and water taxi were all my age while all of the other passengers were my parents' age, no doubt a consequence of the high cost of getting this far from civilization. I talked with the operators about how they'd come across the application for this summer job and had taken it as an opportunity to see Alaska for the season. I wondered to myself what they might have thought of me, on a seemingly frivolous trip to the end of the world for kicks – maybe a trust fund baby? A trip to a private lodge at Lake Clark National Park with my mom left me conscious of this dynamic again. Everyone close to my age was serving the food, tying up the boats, or helping with our luggage while I enjoyed the amenities with the Boomers all around me.

On trains and buses, smoke breaks were the subject of many announcements. On long journeys in vehicles where smoking was expressly prohibited, passengers often asked when the next place they could step off to have a cigarette might be. From its peak a few decades ago, smoking in the public sphere has been curtailed over a very short time horizon. Smoking cigarettes today is largely a phenomenon of the non-college educated crowd (Centers for Disease Control, 2019), making it easy for many college graduates to forget how many of their fellow Americans are as dependent on nicotine as they themselves might be on coffee. I found myself out of place at these smoke breaks, feeling these stops provided an interesting, almost accidental, glimpse into class. They were in their tribe, and I was outside of the tribe – and that was that.

While the socioeconomic differences between travelers and the people who live in the places they are visiting is widely acknowledged, there is often an accompanying cultural dimension, too. On a camping trip with friends up to the Wind River Range in Wyoming, we found a first-come, first-served campsite on National Forest Service land where we spent a couple of nights. Our campground host was an older man sporting a red, white, and blue USA Trucking hoodie, who clocked our out-of-state plates right away. He grumbled how there were way too many people in Colorado now for his liking – and that comment was just about his recent trip to the western part of the state! The Front Range, with its crowded roads and high rents, was a foreign and undesirable world to him. What were his perceptions of us? He never told us, and I didn't ask, so I was left to my imagination.

On a county-counting trip through eastern Kentucky with the friend who'd first introduced me to the Extra Miler Club at the geography conference years earlier, we suffered a mishap – a flat tire on a rural highway. Being city people who may have been book smart but the opposite of handymen, we called Enterprise for help. They linked us to a local tow provider who sent someone out to put on the rental car's spare for us, so we could drive to the closest Enterprise location for a replacement. While we waited for him to arrive, we walked across the state highway to a small restaurant. The local Appalachian accent of the man behind the register was so thick that it was unintelligible to us city folk. We resorted to pointing at the overhead menu, oddly reminiscent of my ordering food in a foreign country. What were his unbridled thoughts of us? When the tow driver arrived, he threw on our spare tire in a matter of minutes while we (two hapless grown men) stood by and watched.

In each of these stories, perceptions of me or the people I was traveling with were never shared directly. After all, we were money-paying customers who expected to be treated with respect. Yet recognizing those subtle changes in body language when judgments are being made, and likely to be shared out loud once you're out of earshot, was something I worked to recognize. I was able to travel the country with all the privileges that come with being a white man in America, and I can't speak to how different my journey might have been if this fact about me had been different. The quiet judgment I did feel was the urban-rural, book smart versus street smart meme. Much in the same way Lightning McQueen is nicknamed "Stickers" in the Pixar movie *Cars* for his general obliviousness to life beyond his racing circuit, I wondered if I might have come across in a similar way to the salt-of-the-earth people I encountered on my travels. If I was Stickers, I'm glad I did finally make it off the interstate to learn more about Radiator Springs and the other places in between.

Danny Zimny-Schmitt

your turn...

Consider how others perceive you

When have you felt judgment being passed on you, either directly or indirectly? Even if there were no words exchanged, how did it make you feel?

If you are a visitor with the economic means to visit someone else's community, how do you think locals might perceive you? Which perceptions do you think might be fair, and which might not be?

Give this some thought, then write your reflections on the next few pages.

Danny Zimny-Schmitt

10 Little Rules for Understanding America

Danny Zimny-Schmitt

10 Little Rules for Understanding America

Danny Zimny-Schmitt

RULE 8
Challenge Your Biases

"It ain't what you don't know that gets you into trouble. It's what you know for sure that just ain't so."

This quote, attributed to Mark Twain, is this chapter in a nutshell. Of the 10 rules in this book, it is the most difficult to follow, because as humans we have a tendency to hold firm to our beliefs even when evidence to the contrary abounds. A political cartoon I first saw in the *Chicago Tribune* in my formative years illustrates this fact well. There are two movie theaters, one showing a film named *An Inconvenient Truth*, the other showing a film named *A Reassuring Lie*; no one stood in line for the former, and everyone was in line for the latter. To build an accurate understanding of the world around us, and specifically the country we call home, we need to continuously seek out new evidence and refine our views. Welcoming new evidence over time allows us to come closer to truths that might make us uncomfortable but will form the basis of a shared path forward in a way that those mutually exclusive, but very reassuring, lies never will.

In Bill Nye's book encouraging us all to think more like objective scientists in everyday lives, "Everything All at Once" (Nye, 2017), he reminds us that double- and triple-checking for the evidence when coming to a conclusion is especially important in instances when that conclusion is something we deeply want to be true. We're likely to throw our hands up and continue the search for evidence when it contradicts our most deeply held beliefs, so approaching the world like a scientist means we always continue the search for more evidence irrespective of how it aligns with our prior beliefs. Before 2016, when I exclusively read books by authors with far-left or center-left viewpoints, it was easy to dismiss evidence from the center or the right because I was systematically excluding ever coming into contact with it. Only when I was ready to open my mind to new evidence did my beliefs start to change.

The combination of my travels and a timely book full of empirical evidence has pushed me to completely transform how I think about rural conservative voters. In their book "The Rural Voter," professors of government Nicholas Jacobs and Daniel Shea compile data on the political views and voting patterns of rural voters compared to their urban and suburban counterparts (Shea & Jacobs, 2023). My baseline view was that rural voters were likely to be the most consistently conservative bloc; after all, rural counties supported Trump by large margins in each of his elections. Yet by dissecting the data on a more granular scale, Jacobs and Shea demonstrate that the most extreme conservative views tend to be held by Republican voters in urban and suburban areas, not rural ones. In a hypothesis describing why this might be the case, they suggest that rural voters might have a better grasp of folks with different ideologies than their own. In smaller rural communities, cross-class interactions happen in a more organic way than in larger metro areas, where residential patterns tend to be more segregated by class. While the local CEO's kid and the local service worker's kid might be teammates on the same team at a high school in small-town New Hampshire, they probably would have never been in the same school district had they grown up south of the state line in metropolitan Massachusetts.

I found this hypothesis quite profound, and I did my best to read the landscape and interrogate whether I could believe it based on what I saw on the ground. Large county high schools abounded across rural America; whenever I drove on weekdays, I saw school buses everywhere ferrying students from all corners of the county to a central high school. Many rural places don't have the population or economic base to support a private school or other class-stratifying institution the way more metropolitan areas do. Thus, evidence on the ground lent support rather than red flags for the book's hypothesis. Based on my own interactions with almost exclusively liberal friends in large cities, where groupthink can be pervasive, it also made sense that conservatives in large cities and suburbs might also fall into groupthink when most of their interactions are with others who may think similarly to the way they do. In the end, I challenged my initial bias that rural voters probably had the most extreme political views and came to believe that urban and suburban voters probably have them beat.

Extremism is just one timely cultural and political issue of our time; another is immigration. I've already recounted the many ways I saw immigrants powering our economy, from those keeping Denver International Airport humming every day to those breathing new life into communities across the Great Plains working in food processing. It was hard not to notice how immigrants are also often working in jobs that are invisibilized; they are more likely to have back-of-the-house roles in the restaurant industry or hold manual labor positions in the agricultural sector. Because so much of the crucial work they do to keep the economy running is behind the scenes, it can be too easy to dismiss their contributions and underestimate just how much might break if they were suddenly removed from their posts. We are at heart a country first founded by immigrants and subsequently populated by many rounds of immigration throughout our history.

So much of the culture war discourse around immigrants zeroes in on whether they broke laws to come to the country or not, when any comprehensive policy conversation needs to center on their role in the economy. Interestingly enough, the role of immigrants in our economy is something that transcends the urban-rural divide, since they work in jobs with slightly different but equally important roles in each context. The country is long overdue for a conversation that moves beyond the too-simple pro- or anti-immigrant mold, challenging the biases on both sides and coming to a consensus that will likely be more closely tied to employment than ideological nonsense about immigrants being welcomed without qualification or being turned away or deported to prove a point. This will absolutely require both sides to compromise on long-held ideological beliefs, something Mark Twain and Bill Nye alike warn will be hard to do.

It's a lot easier to write off large swaths of country as boring nothingness, home to racists, or places to simply pass through on the way to somewhere better. Before setting out on this journey, I admit that I may have been one of those people. In the spirit of interrogating what I might have missed when I held those beliefs, I was curious how people in these places thought about their regions or states being considered "flyover country." To my surprise, many embraced the term as a badge of honor. In downtown Scottsbluff, Nebraska I noticed the new local craft brewery was named Flyover Brewing Company. My friend from South Dakota talked about small-state pride, and how the shared feeling of being overlooked also served as a force to bind people more closely together. Rhetoric from leadership also matters. Running for president in 2020, Senator Amy Klobuchar often repeated that Minnesota isn't flyover country to her; it's home. I found a pride of place almost everywhere I went – and no, most people do not wish to move to the same superstar cities that occupy a disproportionate amount of the national imagination.

I also found myself challenging a myth that long had animated my beliefs as a liberal frustrated with the Electoral College and the Senate granting rural states overrepresentation in our national politics. It went like this: If we could convince just a few hundred thousand out of 39 million blue-voting Californians to move to Wyoming, we could flip two Senate seats to the Democrats overnight! But spending time in rural America made me realize how ridiculous it is to entertain such an idea. People vote not just as individuals but as members of a community, and communities often come to a consensus on which leaders will best serve the economic and political interests of that community. While I cannot prove it because such an experiment hasn't been carried out in real life, I have little doubt that a few hundred thousand relocated

Californians in Wyoming would start voting red as they built new careers and sought out economic opportunities in their new home.

It's a lot easier to dismiss places and the people who live in them when they are just places on a map and not places you've personally visited. It's also easier to leave our biases about such places unchallenged when they remain theoretical rather than integral parts of the country that we've taken the time to contextualize and think about on a human level. To end this rule with a quote from the same man I started it with, I'm going to circle back to something profound Mark Twain said about the act of traveling. "Travel is fatal to prejudice, bigotry, and narrow-mindedness, and many of our people need it sorely on these accounts." While traveling is not guaranteed to challenge your biases or change how you conceptualize the world around you, it is as potent a tool as any out there if you're willing to give it an honest try.

Danny Zimny-Schmitt

your turn...

Challenge your biases

Is there a fervent belief you once held but no longer believe? What evidence made you change your mind?

Think about a belief you currently swear by. Is there anything that would challenge this belief? (Hint: if your answer is no, you may be locking yourself into a biased position.)

Give this some thought and, when you're ready, write down your replies. Remember ... this is a private space so don't be afraid to dig deep.

10 Little Rules for Understanding America

Danny Zimny-Schmitt

10 Little Rules for Understanding America

Danny Zimny-Schmitt

RULE 9
Embrace the Messiness

Weather delays wreaking havoc on flight schedules. Trains and buses running behind schedule or having a weird seat mate on a long journey overland. A hotel looking far grungier in real life than it did online. Questionable fast food, a tense interaction with someone having a bad day, torrential downpours while navigating on unfamiliar highways in an unfamiliar car – we've all experienced the moments that make us want to stay home rather than embrace life on the road. But this messiness is a reminder of the imperfections we'll run into no matter which path we choose. The antidote is not to wall ourselves off from the world so that nothing bad can ever happen to us, but to build up our own resilience so that no matter what hurdle we run into, we have the confidence to overcome it.

No journey of 100,000 miles goes off without any mishaps. The flat tire that stopped us deep in the mountains of eastern Kentucky cost us hours we'd earmarked for seeing more counties later in the day. The missed counties left a hole in my map that I'd have to logistically plan into a future trip. Another flat tire ground me to a halt on a dark desert highway 100 miles north of Las Vegas, necessitating that I stay the night at an old roadside motel because of how far away the closest tow truck was. These misadventures, though inconvenient in the moment, became some of the memories that defined the journey because I was forced into situations that I hadn't planned out on my notepad the night before. Instead, I had to think on my feet. Waiting for the tow all morning in tiny Beatty, Nevada gave me time to check out the local museum featuring the history of the local area, from early mining claims to efforts to oppose the proposed Yucca Mountain national nuclear waste disposal site that had been perpetually planned for the area. At the local grocery store, the cashier asked me to buy a candy bar to support a local youth sports league, mentioning they were part of a statewide contest but never won because of how small their town was next to everyone else in the contest.

My most dramatic experience getting stranded happened somewhere hundreds of miles from the nearest road on the shores of the Arctic Ocean in Barrow, Alaska. Flying Alaska Airlines on a morning flight up from Anchorage, the plan was for a day trip. I'd take a tour of the town and area offered by a local outfitter, dip my toes in the Arctic Ocean, and maybe even see a polar bear from a safe distance. What I didn't know was the moisture and fog of the Arctic summer often makes airplane approaches and landings difficult. In the crowded room that is the Barrow airport, waiting passengers let out a collective groan when the gate agent announced over the PA system that, after two failed approaches, the pilots had turned the plane around to return to Anchorage while they still had enough fuel in the tank to make it back. The next flight out wasn't for another 24 hours, so we shlepped back to the Top of the World Hotel where most of us day trippers had assembled for the tour earlier in the day. A room for the night cost north of $300, and rooms weren't even available until the plane that never arrived returned to Anchorage and passengers called the front desk one by one to cancel their reservations for the night.

It was June, so I waited up until midnight to see the sun shining brightly as the clock struck 12 in the northernmost city in America. The next day, after doing some remote work that I'd intended to handle back at the office, I explored the town and mingled with my fellow stranded travelers – a funny group of older travelers from central Montana, and a father and son from Austin, Texas. The high school-aged son suggested to his dad that maybe he'd apply to Ilisavgik College, the tribal college in town. (We'd learned the day before that each building was equipped with a strobe light that would flash if a polar bear was reported on campus). I wandered into the modern local library, which evidently had just received an influx of investment, and the Inupiat Heritage Center, which focused on the history of whaling amongst the native inhabitants of the area. Reading about how the success of the hunt was believed to be as dependent on the actions of the women responsible for vital tasks around the village as it was on the men out on the whaling boats, I found myself reflecting on how belief systems have to feature a role for everyone. The preeminence of science and objective reality in today's modern age stands in stark contrast to the belief systems that have guided our species for all of its history – and may win out over the cold hard truths of science yet.

On my sojourns across the country, but perhaps especially in the extreme environments of Alaska, I was greatly humbled by coming to understand the profound wisdom of the idiom, "There but for the grace of God go I." Life is fleeting, unfair, and so random in who receives its good fortune and who, through no fault of their own, finds themselves on the sharp edge of fate. While big rigs in the Permian Basin hurtled past my tiny economy rental car, or when I felt my car on the edge of hydroplaning as a storm dumped rain high in the Ouachita Mountains of Arkansas, I did indeed feel how small I was and how lucky I was to be able to make such a journey and come back home in one piece. There is a humility in recognizing not just the physical safety I enjoyed on my journey, but also the economic security that made it possible. Grace delivered me from any messes that would have been too much to overcome.

The messiness of a long journey is not exclusively physical either. When I set out, I expected to come home with lessons that I could neatly break out by state or other well-established designations. Instead, what I learned was that heterogeneity defines many of the things it would be far easier to pack away in summarily defined boxes. States in particular, our most basic units of geography, I found to be particularly poor representations of coherent cultural or political ideas. So many states are better understood as mosaics, comprised of multiple different regions with distinct cultural histories that have been drawn into a single political entity with arbitrary boundaries. These can make understanding a state difficult, since a Pennsylvanian or an Oregonian is not a person you can accurately imagine until you know where in the state they live. (There are also distinct class and racial dimensions to consider; geography plays a part in those, too).

A large state like California is home to perhaps half a dozen distinct regions, from well-known designations like So Cal and the Bay Area to the Central Valley, a huge region with a large population whose more conservative political voice tends to be trampled by the greater numbers living in the state's largest metro areas. Then there are the more lightly populated but distinctive Sierra Nevadas, the inland deserts, and the southern reaches of Cascadia in the state's far north. Depending on where in California someone lives, they may feel more cultural belonging with citizens across the border in Nevada or Oregon than they do with a San Francisco or Orange County resident. The Tennessee license plate famously features three stars that each represent a distinct region of the state: East Tennessee, Middle Tennessee, and West Tennessee. Tennesseans in each of these regions may feel they have more in common with those across state lines in Appalachia, central Kentucky, or the Mississippi Delta region, respectively, than to any coherent marker of identity in their own state. To be sure, some states do have a fairly cohesive sense of identity (think Nebraska, Utah, or Wisconsin), with spillover effects for state-level politics and sports team loyalties alike.

Pondering the randomness of geography and the luck that graced me on my journey at many times left me wondering how my own life might have been different had I ended up or chosen to live in a context different than the one I inhabited. As I explored new cities or flew into airports for a second or third time as I bit off another county-counting adventure heading the opposite direction of the one before it, I began to wonder what my life might be like if I lived somewhere else or inhabited a different reality. Which small city could I see myself being an eligible bachelor in, and which would get claustrophobic? What about raising a family? Did other places strike me as better suited to that? Would retirement be more enjoyable in a small town where everyone knows each other, or would it be stifling? Even if I didn't move my life somewhere, would I enjoy being a traveling businessman who visited Boise, Idaho or Columbus, Georgia, once a month for work? Imagining myself in all these contexts along the way kept me observant and on the lookout for the little details, from local bike paths to vibrant downtowns, that could be regular parts of my life if it took a sudden turn.

Life is messy, and so is traveling. In most situations, from transportation delays to bad weather, we don't have a lot of control over our destinies. Denial and frustration rarely lead anywhere good, and maintaining an open mind may be the best way to avoid pulling out your hair. Instead, let the messy turns become excuses to learn, chances to genuinely connect with the places and people around you. After all, who could empathize better with your plight than someone on the same delayed flight as you? American culture can feel so rushed and hectic all the time. Taking a moment to slow down when fate wills it only ruins your day as much as you allow it to.

Danny Zimny-Schmitt

your turn...

Embrace the messiness

Think back to a travel delay that compromised your original plans. What did you do instead? Did you find a silver lining?

Is there a place you've visited that you found much more complex than you initially anticipated? What surprised you most?

How might you handle a similar situation differently now?

Use the journal pages to write down your thoughts.

Danny Zimny-Schmitt

10 Little Rules for Understanding America

Danny Zimny-Schmitt

10 Little Rules for Understanding America

Danny Zimny-Schmitt

RULE 10
Share What You Learn on the Road

The idea that "With great power comes great responsibility" predates Marvel popularizing it in *Spider-Man* by centuries. It demands that those with privilege in life assume a disproportionate amount of the responsibility for others who may have significantly less. It strikes me as a necessary principle for a healthy society; for as long as we have large gaps in opportunities and outcomes, we need to ask those with more to assume more of the burden. This is not just about the contested arena of taxes and government spending, but also about teaching and sharing with others who haven't had all the advantages in this world that you may have. I admit this is something I have a lot of room for improvement on, and I hope this book is just the start of that work.

Deborah and James Fallows, a couple who made a journey to towns and cities across America with a mission similar to my own, wrote a book by the name of "Our Towns," recounting their travels in their small plane to towns and small cities across the country from coastal Georgia to the inland Northwest (Fallows, 2018). At each stop, they met with local business owners, elected officials, and other community leaders who gave them a rundown of both the success stories and ongoing struggles. Their focus on local economies and how it intertwines with the area's social fabric was more often than not an inspiration, and antidote to the flyover country narrative and the long-term decline of smaller town America. They also noted how riverwalks or similar public spaces can anchor a community around a central point and foster further development and growth, and how "feeling safe" in a place was something they heard again and again from people who wanted to stay in a community for the long run.

So many of the stories they shared rang true with what I also observed, although I didn't meet local leaders to discuss the history of the area and their hopes for its future. The Fallows' approach lent their descriptions a decidedly optimistic outlook – something you'd read in the brochure put out by the local chamber of commerce rather than the sentiment of a longtime resident. While there is nothing wrong with injecting some optimism into the narrative, one of the most important lessons I learned on the road and feel most compelled to share is just how much many Americans and many places are struggling. It's hard not to drive through most counties in the country and wonder when we'd decided that we were going to let most places fall into some state of disrepair, whether that disrepair is limited to the infrastructure itself or is broadened to encompass the economic and social spheres. To be sure, the interviews in "Our Towns" with civic and business leaders are heartwarming, but often came across to me as bold acts of optimism fighting against stronger currents pushing in the opposite direction. This is not meant as a criticism of their work, but rather as a countervailing data point – a lesson I feel the need to share to contribute to this ongoing conversation.

The so-called diploma divide has recently been receiving more attention and with good reason. Those of us with college educations are members of what I'll term a high-risk group for having a poor understanding of America. Because public stories are generally told by people who have college degrees – whether those stories are coming from the media or Hollywood or local officials – college-educated voices are simply heard a lot more than those who don't hold a four-year degree. Compounding this first risk factor is the recognition that our social worlds often don't include many non-college grads, despite the latter group comprising a large majority of the population. It should not come as such a surprise to us when they dissent (especially in elections where they outnumber us), since we've created no other avenues for them to voice their very real concerns.

Sharing what you learn can also be an important exercise in humility, in admitting what you realized you still *don't* know. I am not old enough to be able to compare and contrast how places have changed over time, to witness firsthand whether the past few decades have hit some places much harder than others, or to know if there is real credibility to the idea that the good ol' days really were a better time than today, or if that is just a hollow conservative talking point. It seems likely that the internet has also played a role in changing how we understand America, and I can't recall a world before the internet. Online spaces can quickly descend into shouting matches and insults that seem particularly prone to bringing out the worst in people. Yet was the old town square, where issues were (supposedly) discussed by everyone, that much better, or did complex hierarchies that elevated a few voices over others just result in a different flavor of disagreement? I don't know, but we may find it useful to learn.

Many studies have shown that we are meaner to each other online than we are in face-to-face settings, and I think it's likely these findings have a parallel when it comes to traveling. Isn't it easier to issue summary judgment and be dismissive of people and places we don't know relative to the ones we know well? I admittedly found myself being dismissive of the South as a whole for most of my life before this journey. Taking the time to see the region one county at a time introduced me not only to its natural beauty but also its history and people, who I could sympathize more with up close than from an aloof position far away. I think one of the tragedies of traveling in the US is the lack of affordable hostel accommodations, commonplace in Europe and other places around the world, as they make travel affordable to those who can't afford private hotel rooms. Given that humanizing and fully seeing our fellow citizens often requires meeting them up close, the high cost of travel contributes to why we don't know each other and may be more inclined to judge rather than understand them.

I will close this final chapter with a call to people on both sides of the sociopolitical divides in this country to take a moment to reflect and consider through a different lens one of the views they fervently hold. To those on the left, I ask whether celebrating everyone living out their own truth leads to a positive outcome for society if it also leads to having less common ground and a loss of shared purpose, which are necessary to build lasting bonds and to create something together. To those on the right, I ask you to think about our culture's materialistic tendencies, its celebration of wealth in light of Christ's teaching on poverty, and of the virtue of the poor against the powerful. If I'm doing my job right, at least one of these questions should have made you uncomfortable. We all tell ourselves stories in order to survive, and it is uncomfortable to confront the logical fallacies inherent in our stories. It is only through doing the work of questioning and deeply understanding our own stories, as well as those of others who subscribe to different stories, that we can more fully understand the country we call home. Reading books, traveling through unfamiliar places, and sharing a conversation with someone different from ourselves are the tools we have to do it.

your turn...

Share what you learn on the road

What have you learned while traveling that changed your perspective about something significant?

Did you share your new insight with others?

Do you find that sharing things you learn – whether big or small – comes naturally to you, or is it something that requires more conscious effort to do?

What are some ways you can start to share what you learn while you're away from home?

Danny Zimny-Schmitt

10 Little Rules for Understanding America

Danny Zimny-Schmitt

10 Little Rules for Understanding America

Danny Zimny-Schmitt

CONCLUSION

It is trite to acknowledge that as Americans, we have more in common than what divides us. Many a political stump speech claims we would all find ourselves content if we have the opportunity to live in a safe neighborhood, earn enough money to afford raising children who attend a good school, and get ahead if we work hard and play by the rules. I'm heartened that most people are more moderate than the extremists on either side who make a lot of noise on social media but whose policies are generally unpopular, even with the moderates on their own side. Most Americans appear to want to make politics boring again.

So why can't we get there? The problem, as best I can tell, arises from the all-too-human problem of emotions. How can we make all people feel seen, heard, and respected when there is only so much attention (or public funding) to go around at any given time? It seems likely that a critical mass of people will always feel their opinion or their particular group is not being treated with enough respect. Whether minority groups should have access to affirmative action programs, whether funds should go to build one community's school or another community's road, and where exactly the lines should be drawn between church and state are age-old questions. The myriad valid opinions about each of them also explain why even if we have more that unites us than divides us, political fights among people and groups for limited public funds and public respect alike will always be with us.

To truly understand America, we must be open to having any and all of these challenging conversations, and make an honest effort to listen and understand the views of others. Listen more than you speak. This requires starting from a place of assuming good intention and of seeing everyone as fully human and worthy of respect. Our pluralistic society has always been about compromise. Success is when no one side gets everything they want, but all sides walk away with a solution they can live with; failure is when one side (even when it's your own) does get exactly what they want. Embracing, rather than running away from, the idea that you might be wrong is a powerful – if hard to swallow – force for good. It is humility and compromise, not pride and obstinacy, that will lead us toward a better American tomorrow.

I invite you to use the next several pages to continue exploring the thoughts and feelings you had while reading this book. Think of how you might change the way you move through unfamiliar spaces. Will you be more willing to get off the beaten path, seek out local businesses, talk to strangers, read the landscape? What new rules will you travel by?

This is your space ... and this is your America. Explore!

Danny Zimny-Schmitt

your turn, your rules...

10 Little Rules for Understanding America

10 Little Rules for Understanding America

10 Little Rules for Understanding America

10 Little Rules for Understanding America

10 Little Rules for Understanding America

Danny Zimny-Schmitt

End Notes

Haidt, Jonathan. (2012). *The Righteous Mind: Why Good People are Divided by Politics and Religion*. Pantheon.

Didion, Joan. (1979). *The White Album*. Simon & Schuster.

Brown, Brené. (2017). *Braving the Wilderness*. Random House.

Steinbeck, John. (1980). *Travels with Charley in Search of America*. Penguin Books.

Jones, Matt. (2020). *Mitch, Please! How Mitch McConnell Sold Out Kentucky (and America, Too)*. Simon & Schuster.

Faulkner, William. (1951). *Requiem for a Nun*. Random House.

Terrell, Jessica. (2024) Report Says Home Affordability in Hawaii is 'as bad as it's ever been.' AP News. www.apnews.com. Accessed August 24, 2025.

Fawcett, Eliza. (2023) There's No Ocean in Sight. But Many Hawaiians Make Las Vegas Their Home. Seattle Times. www.seattletimes.com. Accessed August 24, 2025.

Garrett, Martell, Caraballo, King. (2019) Socioeconomic Differences in Cigarette Smoking Among Sociodemographic Groups. Centers for Disease Control. www.cdc.gov. Accessed August 24, 2025.

Nye, Bill. (2017). *Everything all at Once: How to Unleash Your Inner Nerd, Tap Into Radical Curiosity, and Solve Any Problem.* Rodale Books.

Shea, Daniel and Jacobs, Nicholas F. (2023) *The Rural Voter: The Politics of Place and the Disuniting of America.* 2023. Columbia University Press.

Klein, Ezra. (2023) Barbara Kingsolver Thinks Urban Voters Have It All Wrong on Appalachia. The Ezra Klein Show podcast. www.nytimes.com. Accessed August 24, 2025.

Fallows, James and Fallows, Deborah. (2018) *Our Towns: A 100,000-Mile Journey into the Heart of America.* Pantheon.

Acknowledgments

I'd like to acknowledge my geography professors Don Sullivan, Steve Hick, and Andy Goetz, for first showing me that geography could be more than a hobby and then teaching me how to read the landscape and understand the world around me.

Thank you to my friends and co-workers who encouraged me to share the lessons I learned from my travels in a book, and to my editor Carol Pearson for believing in me and in this story.

I'd like to thank my dad, Alan Schmitt, for always encouraging me to observe more and judge less, and my mom, Susan Zimny, for always inspiring me to try my hardest. To my younger brothers Brandon and Ryan: thank you for always putting up with me micromanaging our family vacations.

About the Author

Danny Zimny-Schmitt holds degrees in environmental science and geography from the University of Denver and works in the renewable energy industry. Growing up in inner-city Chicago, visiting family in Wisconsin, and then moving to Denver for school, he was inspired to learn about the differences between places at an early age. When he's not traveling, he enjoys reading, running, and advocacy work for local nonprofits. He lives in Denver.

Connect with Danny and see pix from his latest travels on Instagram @dannyz3142 and Facebook @2danny.zimnyschmitt.

www.ingramcontent.com/pod-product-compliance
Lightning Source LLC
Chambersburg PA
CBHW070626030426
42337CB00020B/3927